Washington F. Friend

The Falls of Niagara

Being a complete guide to all the points of interest around and in the

immediate neighbourhood of the great cataract: with views taken from

sketches by Washington Friend, Esq., and from photographs

Washington F. Friend

The Falls of Niagara
*Being a complete guide to all the points of interest around and in the immediate
neighbourhood of the great cataract: with views taken from sketches by
Washington Friend, Esq., and from photographs*

ISBN/EAN: 9783337373368

Printed in Europe, USA, Canada, Australia, Japan

Cover: Foto ©Lupo / pixelio.de

More available books at **www.hansebooks.com**

THE

FALLS OF NIAGARA:

BEING

A Complete Guide to all the Points of
Interest around and in the Immediate Neighbourhood
of the Great Cataract.

WITH

VIEWS TAKEN FROM SKETCHES BY WASHINGTON FRIEND, ESQ.,
AND FROM PHOTOGRAPHS.

THE RAPIDS ABOVE THE FALLS.

T. NELSON & SONS, LONDON, EDINBURGH, & NEW YORK
TORONTO: JAMES CAMPBELL.

MDCCCLX.

INDEX.

NIAGARA FALLS
AND VICINITY

NIAGARA RIVER,
FROM
LAKE ERIE TO LAKE ONTARIO

FALLS OF NIAGARA.

INTRODUCTION.

THE Falls of Niagara may justly be classed among the wonders of the world. They are the pride of America, unequalled in grandeur, magnitude, and magnificence, by any other known cataract; and have, since they were discovered, exerted an attractive influence over millions of the human race, who have flocked thither year after year to gaze upon that tumultuous crash of water with feelings of the deepest solemnity. The power and majesty of the Almighty are, perhaps, more awfully exhibited and more fully realized in this stupendous waterfall than in any other scene on earth.

In the following pages we shall attempt to guide the traveller to the various points whence the finest views of the Falls may be obtained, and, thereafter, conduct him to the spots of peculiar interest in their neighbourhood.

The great lakes of North America—Superior, Michigan, Huron and Erie—pour the flood of their accumulated waters into Lake Ontario through a channel of about 36 miles in length. This channel is named the

Niagara River, and is part of the boundary between Canada and the state of New York. Twenty-two miles below its commencement at Lake Erie occur the famous Falls of Niagara. These Falls are divided into two by Iris or Goat Island. The American Falls are 900 feet wide, by 163 feet high. The Horse-Shoe or Canadian Fall is 2000 feet wide, and 154 feet high. The origin of the name is uncertain, but it is supposed to be of Iroquois extraction, and to signify the "Thunder of Waters." The roar of the Falls is sometimes heard at a great distance, but of course it is constantly modified by the direction and strength of the wind. Over this magnificent precipice the irresistible tide rushes at the rate of 100 million tons of water every hour! It is computed that the precipice is worn away by the friction of the water at the rate of about one foot a-year, and it is believed that the Falls have gradually receded from Queenston, seven miles below, to their present position. The river above the Falls is studded with islands of all sizes, amounting to 37 in number. The width of the stream varies from several hundred yards to three miles. At the Falls it is about three-quarters of a mile wide. The total descent from Lake Erie to Ontario is 334 feet. So much for statistics.

The Falls of Niagara were first seen by a white man 180 years ago. *Father Hennepin*, a French Jesuit missionary, first saw them when on an expedition of discovery in the year 1678.

The spots of interest to be visited, besides the great Fall itself, are :—The Ground where the memorable Battle of Lundy's Lane was fought ; the Whirlpool below the Falls ; the Suspension Bridges ; the Devil's Hole and the Bloody Run ; the Queenston Heights and General Brock's Monument, &c.

We think it right to say that the Engravings with which our work is embellished may be depended on as being minutely correct, the most of them having been copied from photographs, and others taken from drawings made on the spot by Washington Friend, Esq., whose beautiful and cleverly executed panorama of American scenery is so well known to the public, and which is now exhibiting in England.

———

Let us suppose, then, reader, that you have reached the Falls on the American side ; that you have just alighted from the train in the Village of the Falls, and the thunder of Niagara is sounding in your ears. It were superfluous to give you minute directions how to proceed. Follow the crowd and you cannot go wrong; there are also numerous ready and efficient guides, and, were these lacking, the roar of the great cataract would of itself be sufficient.

2

The Village of the Falls, through which you pass, lies on the east side of the river, in the immediate vicinity of the grand cataract, 22 miles by rail from the town of Buffalo on Lake Erie, and 300 by rail from Albany. Being a fashionable place of resort during summer and autumn. *The Hotels* at this village are excellent in all respects, and most agreeable abodes for those who intend to sojourn for a time within sound of the Falls. The chief of them are the *Cataract House* and the *International Hotel*, in which the accommodation and entertainment will be found quite equal to that on the Canada side. The *Monteagle Hotel* is near the Suspension Bridge, 2 miles further down the river. Conveyances may be had from the above hotel to all parts of Niagara. But we are too near the Falls to linger here. Pushing forward down the street leading between the two hotels just mentioned, we come into full view of the river at the point where it is spanned by the

SUSPENSION BRIDGE ABOVE THE RAPIDS.

Here the first perceptions of power and grandeur begin to awaken in our minds. The noble river is seen hurrying on towards its final leap; and as we stand upon the bridge looking down upon the gushing flood of water, that seems as if it would sweep away our frail standing ground and hurl us over the dread precipice

whose rounded edge is but a few yards farther down, we begin, though feebly as yet, to realize the immensity of this far-famed cataract. This is the finest point of view from which to observe the *rapids above the Falls.* The fall of the river from the head of the rapids (a mile above the Falls) to the edge of the precipice is nearly 60 feet; and the tumultuous madness of the waters, hurling and foaming in wayward billows and breakers down this descent, as if fretting with impatience, is a fine contrast to the uniform magnificent sweep with which at length they gush into the thundering flood below.

At the other end of the bridge, as seen in our Engraving, is *Bath Island,* on which is the *Toll-house,* where each visitor is charged 25 cents, and has his name entered in a book; after which he is entitled to cross the bridge as often as he pleases, free of charge, during the current year. Bath Island is connected with *Iris* or *Goat Island* by another bridge; and beyond Goat Island there are a few scattered rocks, which are connected with it by means of a third bridge. These rocks lie on the very brink of the precipice, between the *American* Falls and the *Horse-Shoe* Fall, and on them stands a tower named the *Terrapin Tower,* which commands a magnificent view of Niagara. But there are finer points of view than this. Moreover, we shall afterwards have to conduct our reader to various points of great interest on and around these islands, which, however, no one will feel disposed to visit until he has given his undivided attention to the wonderful Falls from the most striking points of view. We therefore recommend him not to cross over to Goat Island in the first instance, but, after having stood upon the bridge over the rapids above described, retrace his steps and hasten down the banks of the river a few hundred yards, to a spot named *Prospect Point.*

Before proceeding thither, however, we may say a word or two in reference to the bridge we are about to leave. The elegant and substantial structure that now spans the river at this point was erected by the Messrs. Porter, the proprietors of Goat Island. It is made or iron, on the plan of Whipple's iron-arched bridge, and is 360 feet long, having 4 arches of 90 feet span each. The width is 27 feet, embracing a double carriage-way of 16½ feet, and two foot-paths of 5¼ feet each, with iron railings. All the materials used in its construction are of the best quality, and the strength of all the parts is much beyond what is considered necessary.

The first bridge that was thrown over these turbulent waters was constructed at the head of Goat Island in 1817. It was carried away by ice in the following spring, and was succeeded by another, which was built in 1818. The difficulties attending its construction were overcome in the following manner: A mas-

sive abutment of timber was built at the water's edge, from which were projected enormously long and heavy beams of timber. These beams were secured on the land side by heavy loads of stone, and their outer ends were rendered steady by means of stilts or legs let down from them and thrust into the bottom of the river. A platform was thrown over this projection, along which heavy masses of stone were carried and dropped into the river. This operation was continued until the heap appeared above water, and then a strong framework of timber, filled solidly with stone, was built upon it. To this pier the first permanent portion of the bridge was fixed, and then, commencing from the extremity, beams were run out and a second pier similarly formed, and so on till the bridge was completed. It was built by the Messrs. Porter—extensive proprietors in this neighbourhood—and was repaired in 1839, and again in 1849.

In the former year one of the workmen, named Chapin, fell from the bridge into the river; fortunately the current carried him to the first of the two small islets below. He was rescued from his perilous position by Mr. J. R. Robinson, who has more than once bravely rescued fellow-creatures from this dangerous river; and the island was named after him—Chapin Island.

In July 1853, another accident occurred near this

point. Two Germans took a boat, and set out for a pleasure sail on the river above the Falls. Nothing more was heard of them until next morning, when one of them, named Joseph Avery, was observed clinging to a log sticking in the midst of the rapids, near the bridge between Bath Island and the mainland. Thousands of people assembled to render the poor man assistance, and during the day various attempts were made to rescue him from his perilous position, but without success. At length a boat was lowered down the rapids toward the log to which he clung. It neared him, and he attempted to spring towards it; but his strength was gone, and he fell into the stream. In another moment he was swept over the Falls. His body was never found.

NIAGARA FALLS FROM PROSPECT POINT.

This is indeed a sight worth coming many hundred miles to see. Walking through the Grove, we emerge upon the Point in front of Prospect Point Cottage. Here, at one wide sweep, we behold Niagara stretching from the American to the Canadian side in magnificent perspective. Just at our feet the smooth deep masses of the American Falls undulate convulsively as they hurl over the precipice and dash, in a never-ending succession of what we may term passionate bursts, upon the rugged rocks beneath. Beyond, and a little to the left, is Goat

Island, richly clothed with trees, its drooping end seeming as if it, too, were plunging, like the mighty river, into the seething abyss. Just off the Point is seen the Terrapin Tower, and right in front of us is the great Horse-Shoe Fall, uttering its deep, deafening roar of endless melody, as it plunges majestically into that curdling sea, from which the white cloud of mist spouts high in air and partially conceals the back ground of Canada from view. Far down in the river below, the ferryboats are seen dancing on the angry waters. It is a solemnizing prospect, and we should suppose that few could gaze upon it for the first time without feeling that they had attained to a higher conception of the awful power and might of the Eternal. This point was the last residence of Francis Abbot, the young Hermit of Niagara.

The American Fall, on the brink of which we stand, is 163 feet in perpendicular height, and 660 feet wide from the mainland to *Luna* Island. The smaller Fall, between Luna and Goat Island, is 240 feet wide. Within a short distance of the spot where we stand is the

FERRY HOUSE.

Here there is a curious inclined plane, down which we descend in cars, which are worked by means of a water wheel and a rope ; there is also a stair connected with this, at the foot of which the ferry-boat waits to convey us over to the Canadian side, whither we intend to proceed, because one of the finest views of Niagara is had from *Table Rock.* Ten minutes will suffice to convey us over, and the passage is quite safe. The charge is 18¾ cents; but before going, let us hasten to the foot of the *American Falls,* and view them *from below.*

Mr. Charles Dickens, writing of this scene, says: "The bank is very steep, and was slippery with rain and half-melted ice. I hardly know how I got down, but I was soon at the bottom, and climbing with two English officers, who were crossing and had joined me, over some broken rocks, deafened by the noise, half-blinded by the spray, and wet to the skin, we were at the foot of the American Fall. I could see an immense torrent of water tearing headlong down from some great height, but had no idea of shape or situation, or anything but vague immensity."

Seating ourselves in the Ferry boat, we are soon dancing on the agitated waters, and gazing in profound silence and admiration at the Falls, which from this point of view are seen to great advantage. A few minutes, and we are standing on the soil of Canada. Here carriages are ready to convey us to Table Rock, little more than a mile distant. Clifton House, not far from the landing, and several other objects of interest, claim our attention; but we are too full of the Great Cataract just now to turn aside, and, as we shall pass this way again in descending the river, we will hasten on to behold the sublime view of Niagara from

TABLE ROCK.

In alluding to this view, the graphic writer above quoted says : " It was not till I came on Table Rock, and looked on the fall of bright green water, that it came upon me in its full might and majesty. Then Niagara was for ever stamped upon my heart, an image of beauty, to remain there, changeless and indelible, until its pulses cease to beat for ever.

" Oh, how the strife and trouble of daily life receded from my view and lessened in the distance, during the ten memorable days we passed on that enchanted ground ! What voices spake from out the thundering water ! what faces, faded from the earth, looked out upon me from its gleaming depths ! what heavenly pro- mise glistened in those angels' tears, the drops of many hues, that showered around, and twined themselves about the gorgeous arches which the changing rainbows made ! . . . To wander to and fro all day, and see the cataract from all points of view ; to stand upon the edge of the Great Horse-Shoe Fall, marking the hurried water gathering strength as it approached the verge, yet seeming, too, to pause before it shot into the gulf below ; to gaze from the river's level up at the torrent as it came streaming down ; to climb the neighbouring

B   3

heights and watch it through the trees, and see the
wreathing water in the rapids hurrying on to take its
fearful plunge; to linger in the shadow of the solemn
rocks three miles below, watching the river as, stirred
by no visible cause, it heaved, and eddied, and awoke
the echoes, being troubled yet, far down beneath the
surface, by its giant leap; to have Niagara before me,
lighted by the sun and by the moon, red in the day's
decline and gray as evening slowly fell upon it; to look
upon it every day, and wake up in the night and hear
its ceaseless voice: this was enough.

"I think in every quiet season now, Still do those
waters roll and leap, and roar and tumble, all day long;
still are the rainbows spanning them a hundred feet
below; still, when the sun is on them, do they shine
and glow like molten gold; still, when the day is
gloomy, do they fall like snow, or seem to crumble away
like the front of a great chalk cliff, or roll down the rock
like dense white smoke. But always does the mighty
stream appear to die as it comes down, and always from
its unfathomable grave arises that tremendous ghost of
spray and mist which is never laid: which has haunted
this place with the same dread solemnity since darkness
brooded on the deep, and that first flood before the
deluge—light—came rushing on creation at the word of
God."

But no words, however appropriate, no combination

From a Photograph

of ideas, however felicitous, can do justice to Niagara ; and those who are wending their way thither will need no description : yet it is satisfactory to know the feelings and thoughts of those who have gone before us.

Table Rock is no longer the extensive platform that it once was, large portions of it having fallen from time to time. It overhangs the terrible caldron close to the Horse-Shoe Fall, and the view from it, as already described, is most sublime. In 1818 a mass of 160 feet long and 40 feet wide broke off and fell into the boiling flood; and in 1828 three immense masses fell with a shock like an earthquake. Again, in 1829, another fragment fell, and in 1850 a portion of about 200 feet in length and 100 feet thick. On one of these occasions some forty or fifty persons had been standing on the rock a few minutes before it fell! The work of demolition still goes on, for another portion of Table Rock fell last year (1857).

Standing on the verge of Table Rock, and looking down into that angry swirl of mist and heaving waters, we behold a steamboat battling with the flood. It is

THE MAID OF THE MIST.

This little steamer starts from the landing, close to the Suspension Bridge, two miles below Niagara, and, ascending the river, passes the American Falls, and penetrates boldly into the dense cloud of mist close to the foot of the Horse-Shoe Fall. This two-miles' trip is of a most thrilling character. Passing between the steep cliffs on each side of the river, we obtain a magnificent view of the whole line of the Falls in all positions, until everything is shut out from our sight by the drenching spray, as we dash, to all appearance, into the very jaws of the roaring cataract. But the Maid of the Mist wheels gracefully round in time, and emerges from the white curtain, glittering in the diamond drops which she has snatched from the rainbows of Niagara! Water-proof garments are provided, free of charge, for those who wish to remain on deck during the trip. There is no real danger attending this excursion. The steamer was built expressly for her present work, and she is an excellent boat of 170 tons burden, and propelled by an engine of above 100 horse-power. The Maid of the Mist makes hourly trips every day except Sundays.

A short distance from Table Rock there is a stair by which we can descend under the overhanging cliff, and if we desire it, don the waterproof habiliments provided for us, and go under

THE HORSE SHOE FALL

The view here is awfully grand. As we gaze upwards at the frowning cliff that seems tottering to its fall, and pass under the thick curtain of water—so near that it seems as if we could touch it—and hear the hissing

HORSE SHOE FALL

spray, and are stunned by the deafening roar that issues from the misty vortex at our feet, an indescribable feeling of awe steals over us, and we are more than ever impressed with the tremendous magnificence of Niagara.

VIEW BELOW TABLE ROCK.

Behind our narrow foot-path the precipice of the Horse-Shoe Fall rises perpendicularly to a height of 90 feet; at our feet the cliff descends about 70 feet into a turmoil of bursting foam; in front is the liquid curtain which, though ever passing onward, never unveils this wildest of Nature's caverns.

We do not run much danger in going under the Falls if we are moderately careful, and hundreds of ladies do so every year. But accidents have happened more than once to reckless travellers. To the nervous and the timid we would say, go under the Falls by all means, and *fear not;* to the daring and the bold we would say go, but *beware.* At the same time it is right to mention that portions of Table Rock are still expected to fall every year, so that those who go under the Falls must run the risk of this.

The volume of water that gushes over the Horse-Shoe Fall is enormous. It is estimated that the sheet is fully 20 feet thick in the centre, an estimate which was corroborated in a singular manner in 1829. A ship named the *Detroit*, having been condemned, was bought and sent over the Falls. On board were put a live bear, a deer, a buffalo, and several smaller animals. The vessel was almost knocked to pieces in the rapids, but a large portion of her hull went over entire. She drew 18 feet water, but did not strike the cliff as she took the awful plunge.

PROSPECT HOUSE

Stands in the rear of Table Rock. The view from the summit of this building is magnificent.

THREE SISTERS & GOAT ISLAND FROM CANADA SIDE.

A few hundred yards above Prospect House there is a point from which we obtain a fine view of the rapids and the islands named

THE THREE SISTERS.

They are seen in the distance lying close together at the head of Goat Island.

From one of these Sisters a gentleman named Allan was rescued by the gallant Mr. J. R. Robinson in the summer of 1841. Mr. Allan had started alone in his boat for the village of Chippewa, and in the middle of the river broke one of his oars. Being unable to gain the shore, he endeavoured with the remaining oar to steer for the head of Goat Island, but the rapid current swept him past this point. As he approached the outer island of the Three Sisters, he steered with the cool energy of despair towards it and leaped ashore, while his boat sprang like a lightning flash down the rapid and over the Horse-Shoe Fall. For two days Mr. Allan remained on the island, and then, fortunately, succeeded in making a fire with some matches he happened to have in his pocket. Crowds of people assembled to assist in and witness the rescue, which was accomplished by Robinson, who, having managed to pass a rope from island to island, reached him with a skiff.

Another narrow escape was made here by a father and son in the year 1850. The son, a boy of ten years of age, was paddling his father—who was drunk at the time—over to their home on Grand Island. The father was unable to guide the frail canoe, which was carried into the rapids, and descended with fearful rapidity towards the Falls. The wretched father could do nothing to save himself; but the gallant boy struggled with the energy of a hero, and succeeded in forcing the canoe between Goat Island and the Three Sisters. Here they were in imminent danger of passing over the little cascade between these islands, but, providentially, as they neared it a wave upset the canoe and left them struggling in the water. The place was shallow,—the boy gained a footing, and, seizing his father by the collar, dragged him to the shore, where hundreds of anxious spectators received them with shouts of joy.

Gull Island is a small island just above the Horse-Shoe Fall. It has never been trodden by man.

About two miles higher up the river is

THE BURNING SPRING.

This curious spring is very interesting. The water, being charged with sulphureted hydrogen gas, takes fire when a light is applied to it, and burns with a pale, bluish flame.

The Battle of Chippewa was fought in this neighbourhood on the 5th July, 1814.

In order to gratify the visitor's natural desire to see

AMERICAN FALLS.

Niagara from the most striking points of view, we have hurried him somewhat abruptly to the Canada side. We will now retrace our steps to the Ferry, and, crossing over, visit Goat Island and its neighbourhood.

The first object that claims our attention as we return down the left bank of the river is

THE MUSEUM,

Which stands at the top of the bank near to Table Rock, and is well worth visiting. It is arranged so as to represent a forest scene, and contains a fine collection of birds, beasts, and fishes, besides a camera-obscura. Charge for admission 25 cents.

A short distance below this house a terrible accident occurred in 1844. A lady named Miss Martha K. Rugg fell over the bank, and, descending a depth of 115 feet, was dashed on the sharp rocks below. She was still alive when picked up, but expired a few hours afterwards.

Our Engraving of the

AMERICAN FALLS

Exhibits the view as seen from the Canadian side directly opposite. Behind the Falls are seen the splendid American Hotels, the Cataract House, the International, &c., with the woods extending towards Prospect Point. On the right are the Centre Fall and the wooden stairs leading to the Cave of the Winds.

4

From this position we have also a fine prospect of

NIAGARA RIVER BELOW THE FALLS.

Our Engraving, taken from a photograph, gives an excellent and correct representation of this view. The swollen and agitated stream hurries onward, after its mighty leap, between steep cliffs, clothed on the summit with wood. On the left of the Picture we see the road winding along the top of the bank towards the splendid hotel named Clifton House; groups of pilgrims to the shrine of the mighty cataract of the West enliven the scene, and, perchance, the Ferry boat shoots out from its moorings as we pass, and dances like a cork upon the troubled waters.

A walk of about half an hour along the bank of the river, brings us to

CLIFTON HOUSE,

A magnificent hotel, in the immediate vicinity of which is the ground where the *Battle of Lundy's Lane* was fought. It occupies a commanding position on the top of the bank, at a short distance from the Ferry Landing-Place. The view of the American and Horse-Shoe Falls from this hotel is exceedingly fine, and the accommodation is excellent. The gardens around it are a great improvement, and it has concert rooms, large

From a Photograph.

public saloons, and is lighted with gas. The Erie and Ontario Railroad, which passes close to it, connects at Chippewa, a village about three miles up the river, with the steamer to Buffalo, and runs down the river to the City of Niagara, at its mouth, whence the Lake Ontario steamers convey passengers to the River St. Lawrence.

Having thus cast a rapid glance at the salient points on the Canada side, we may either continue our walk for a mile further, to the Suspension Bridge, or recross the Ferry to inspect the Falls more narrowly. Choosing the latter course, we cross in the boat, re-ascend the inclined-plane railway, hurry through the Grove, and cross the bridge to

BATH ISLAND.

Here is a bathing establishment, having warm and plunge baths open at all hours of the day; and here also may be purchased any amount of Indian curiosities. The largest paper mill in the United States is also on this island. It belongs to Bradley and Co. of Buffalo. A little higher up are two smaller islets named *Ship* and *Brig* Islands. The former is also named *Lovers' Retreat*, and is connected with Bath Island by a slender but safe bridge. Looking down the river we see several small islets, most of which are more or less connected with thrilling incidents of danger, escape, or death; for graphic details of which we refer the traveller to the guides, who are learned in local tradition.

Crossing the bridge at the other end of Bath Island, we reach

GOAT, OR IRIS ISLAND.

This island is half a mile long by a quarter broad, and contains about 70 acres. It divides the Falls, is 330 yards wide, and is heavily wooded. In 1770 a man of the name of Stedman placed some goats here to pasture; hence the name. Its other name, Iris, is derived from the number of beautiful rainbows that are so frequently seen near it. It is the property of the Porter family, and to them the public are indebted for the facilities which are afforded them in visiting the Falls. Goat Island was visited long before the bridges were constructed; but the visitors were not numerous, the risk being very great. The dates 1771, 1772, and 1779, under the names of several strangers, were found cut in a beech tree near the Horse-Shoe Fall.

Three paths diverge from the house on your left, in which Indian curiosities are sold; the one to the left leads to the head of the island; the centre road cuts right across it; and that on the right conducts to the Falls. Let us follow the latter through the trees that line the margin of the rapids. In a few minutes we reach a spot named *Hog's Back*, from which we have a good view of the Central and American Falls and the river below, rushing on as if in exultation after its terrific leap. Dr. Hungerford of West Troy was killed just under this point in 1839, by the falling of a portion of the cliff.

Three Profiles, formed by the Falls in this neighbourhood, are pointed out, but they exist chiefly in the imagination!

That small island to our right, on the verge of the Falls, is

LUNA ISLAND;

So called because it is the best point from which to view the beautiful *Lunar Bow*. A narrow bridge connects this island with Goat Island.

The *Lunar Bow* is only seen once a-month, when the moon is full and sufficiently high in the heavens.

The *Solar Bow* is always visible when the sun shines on the Falls.

It is said by some that Luna Island trembles; which is not improbable.

A very melancholy accident occurred at the northern extremity of this island in the year 1849. The family of Mr. Deforest of Buffalo visited the Falls on the 21st June of that year, along with a young man named Charles Addington. They were about to leave this island when Mr. Addington playfully seized Annette, the little daughter of Mr. Deforest, in his arms, and held her over the edge of the bank, exclaiming, " I am going to throw you in." A sudden impulse of fear caused the child to bound from his grasp and fall into the rushing stream: with a loud cry of horror the young man sprang in to save her, and, ere the stricken parents could utter a cry, they both went over the Falls! In the afternoon the mangled remains of the child were discovered in the Cave of the Winds, but Addington's body was not found for several days afterwards.

THE CENTRE FALL,

Over which we pass in our return to Goat Island, although a mere ribbon of white water when seen from a short distance in contrast with the Great Falls, is by no means unworthy of notice. It is 240 feet wide, and is a very graceful sheet of water. Proceeding along the road a short distance, we come to

BIDDLE'S STAIRS.

These were erected in 1829 by Mr. Biddle, president of the United States' Bank, for the purpose of enabling visitors to descend the perpendicular precipice. The stairs are firmly secured to the cliff, and are said to be quite safe. They are 80 feet high. The total descent from the top of the bank to the bottom is 185 feet.

Between this point and the Centre Fall is the spot where the celebrated *Sam Patch* made his famous leaps. Sam made two leaps in 1829. A long ladder was placed at the foot of the rock and fastened with ropes in such a manner that the top projected over the water. A platform was then laid from the top of the ladder to the edge of the bank above. Hundreds of thousands of spectators crowded every point within sight of the place on both shores, eager to behold the extraordinary spectacle of a man jumping "over the Falls." Sam walked along the giddy platform, made his bow, and went down, feet first, 97 feet into the river.

Not content with this achievement, Sam Patch afterwards made a higher leap at the Genesee Falls. Again, at the same place, he made another jump, from the height of 125 feet! This was his last. The poor fellow never rose again, and his body has never been found.

Before descending Biddle's Stairs, let us pass on until we reach the extremity of the island, and cross the bridge to

TERRAPIN TOWER.

This tower occupies a singular and awful position. A few scattered masses of rock lie on the very brink of the Great Fall, seeming as if unable to maintain their position against the tremendous rush of water. Upon these rocks the tower is built. It was erected in 1833, by Judge Porter; and from the summit we obtain the most magnificent view that can be conceived,—the rapids above rolling tumultuously towards you,—the green water of the mighty Falls at your feet,—below you the hissing caldron of spray, and the river with its steep banks beyond,—in fact the whole range of the Falls themselves, and the world of raging waters around them, are seen from this commanding point of view. The tower is 45 feet high.

The bridge leading to this tower is usually wet with spray, so that we must be careful in crossing. In 1852 a gentleman fell from this bridge, and was carried to the edge of the Fall; fortunately he stuck between two rocks, and was rescued by two Americans, who threw lines towards him, which he fastened round his body, and was thus drawn ashore.

A timber which projects over the dread abyss was the usual evening promenade of the eccentric Francis Abbot. In 1852 two enormous pieces of the precipice here, reaching from the top to the bottom, broke off and fell with a crash like thunder.

While gazing at the sublime sight here, and taking in at a single sweep the whole scene of the glorious Falls of Niagara, let us pause a while and reflect upon the sad fate of

FRANCIS ABBOT, THE HERMIT OF THE FALLS.

In the month of June 1829, a tall, gentlemanly, but haggard-looking young man, made his appearance at the Village of the Falls. He brought with him a large portfolio and several books and musical instruments. For a few weeks he paid daily and nightly visits to the most interesting points of Niagara, and at length became so fascinated with the beauty and sublimity of the scene, that he resolved to take up his abode there altogether! No one knew whence the young stranger came. Those who conversed with him asserted that he was talented and engaging in his manners and address; but he was not communicative, and shunned the company of man. At the end of a few weeks he applied for permission to build for himself a cottage on one of the Three Sisters; but circumstances preventing this, he took up his residence in an old cottage on Goat Island. Here the young hermit spent his days and nights in solitary contemplation of the great cataract; and when winter came, the dwellers on the mainland saw the twinkle of his wood-fire, and listened wonderingly to the sweet tones of music that floated over the troubled waters and mingled with the thunder of the Falls.

This wonderful recluse seemed never to rest. At all hours of the day and night he might be seen wandering round the object of his adoration. Not content with gazing at the rapids, he regularly bathed in the turbulent waters, and the bathing-place of Francis Abbot is still pointed out to visitors. At the Terrapin Bridge there is a single beam of timber which projects its tremulous end about ten feet over the roaring flood. Along this the hermit was in the habit of walking. He did so without the smallest sign of fear,—with a firm, bold

C

step proceeding to the very end, turning on his heel and walking back again. One day in June 1831 he went to bathe in the river below the Falls. Not long afterwards his clothes were found still lying on the bank, but Francis Abbot was gone. The waters which he had so recklessly dared had claimed him as their own at last. His body was found ten days afterwards at the mouth of the river, whence it was conveyed to Niagara and buried close to the thundering Fall he loved so well.

Returning to *Biddle's Stairs*, let us descend, and, taking the road to the left, go view the

HORSE-SHOE FALL FROM BELOW GOAT ISLAND.

The sight is terrific. The frowning cliff seems about to fall on us, and we are stunned by the roar of the water as it falls headlong on the broken rocks, bursts into white foam, and re-ascends in clouds of spray. Terrapin Bridge and Tower, now diminished by distance, seem about to be swept over the Fall, above the edge of which we see the trees of Canada. Portions of the rock fall here occasionally, so that the passage is not altogether unattended with danger.

Returning to the foot of the stairs, we follow the road to the right until we reach the famous

CAVE OF THE WINDS.

It is situated at the foot of the rock between Goat and Luna Islands, and is considered by some to be one of the finest and most wonderful sights on the American side. Here it is necessary to put on waterproof dresses and obtain a guide—both of which are at all times at our command. The cave has been formed by the action of the water on the soft substratum of the precipice, which has been washed away and the limestone rock left arching overhead 30 feet beyond the base. In front the transparent Falls form a beautiful curtain. In consequence of the tremendous pressure on the atmosphere, this cave is filled with perpetual storms, and the war of conflicting elements is quite chaotic. A beautiful *rainbow*, quite circular in form, quivers amid the driving spray when the sun shines. The cave is 100 feet wide, 130 feet high, and upwards of 30 feet deep. Along the floor of this remarkable cavern the spray is hurled with considerable violence, so that it strikes the walls and curls upwards along the ceiling, thus causing the rough turmoil which has procured for this place its title of the Cave of the Winds. It is much visited by ladies as well as gentlemen, and a good railing has been put up, as well as one or two seats, by the proprietor.

Re-ascending Biddle's Stairs we will now proceed to the

HEAD OF GOAT ISLAND.

The road runs quite round it. Turning to the right, in the direction of Terrapin Bridge, we observe that the rock is wearing away fast here. In 1843 an enormous mass fell from the precipice with a tremendous crash, and the rock lies near the foot of the stairs.

Passing on along the edge of the rapids, we come to the *Three Sisters*, (already described); and here, between *Moss Island* and the shore, is a small but beautiful Fall, named the *Hermit's Cascade*. Hither the unfortunate Abbot was wont to repair daily to enjoy a shower-bath of Nature's own constructing. Proceeding onwards, we reach the head of Iris Island and the cottage in which Abbot lived before removing to his last residence, at Prospect Point.

In June of 1854 Mr. Robinson performed a daring feat here. A sand-scow, or flat-bottomed barge, having broken loose from its moorings, lodged on the rocks near the head of the island. There was property on board which Mr. Robinson offered to save. Embarking with his son in a skiff, he shot out into the rapid, and was carried with terrible swiftness down towards the scow, upon which the son sprang as they flew past, and very cleverly fastened the skiff to it. Having obtained the goods for which they ran so great risk, the fearless pair pushed off once more, and flew like an arrow on the surging billows towards the Three Sisters. Every one thought their doom was sealed, for they were flying towards the small cascade, to go over which would have been certain death. But, on its very verge they swept adroitly into an eddy, and succeeded in gaining the second

Sister. Here they carried their skiff to the foot of the island, where they launched it, and, plying their oars with vigour, made a bold sweep down the rapids, and gained the shore of Goat Island in safety.

The view from the head of Goat Island is very fine, the wild river and its environs being seen for a considerable distance. Navy Island, celebrated in the history of border warfare; the site of old Fort Schlosser on the American side; the town of Chippewa on the Canada shore; Grand Island, &c., are all visible from this point. As we gaze at the wild rapid, we wonder at the hardihood of those who ventured to descend to the spot on which we now stand before the bridge was built. Yet this was occasionally done, at much risk, in Indian canoes. It is said that any one who falls into the rapids a mile above the Falls is hurried to almost certain destruction; and there are many melancholy instances of the kind.

A few years ago an Indian attempted, while in a state of partial intoxication, to cross the river in his canoe. He was drawn into the rapids, and, despite his utmost efforts, failed to reach the shore. Knowing that his doom was fixed, he took a draught of spirits, and then, lying down at full length in the canoe, was hurled over the Falls into eternity.

In proceeding down the island we pass a spot where there are several graves, out of which human remains have been dug. They were found in a sitting position, and it is supposed they were those of the ancient Indian warriors who first owned the land around the Falls.

NIAGARA IN WINTER.

In all its phases this wondrous cataract is sublime, but in winter, when its dark-green waters contrast with the pure white snow, and its frosty vapour spouts up into the chill atmosphere from a perfect chaos of ice and foam, there is a perfection of savage grandeur about it which cannot be realized in the green months of summer.

At this season ice is the ruling genius of the spot. The spray which bursts from the thundering cataract encrusts every object with a coat of purest dazzling white. The trees bend gracefully under its weight, as if in silent homage to the Spirit of the Falls. Every twig is covered, every bough is laden; and those parts of the rocks and trees on which the delicate frost-work will not lie, stand out in bold contrast. At the foot of the Falls block rises on block in wild confusion, and the cold, dismal-looking water, hurries its green floods over the brink, and roars hoarsely as it rushes into the vortex of dazzling white below. The trees on Goat Island seem partially buried; the bushes around have almost disappeared; the houses seem to sink under their ponderous coverings of white; every rail is edged with it, every point and pinnacle is capped with it; and the dark form

NIAGARA IN WINTER FROM CANADA SIDE.

of the Terrapin Tower stands like a lone sentinel guarding this scene of magnificent desolation.

When the sun shines, all becomes radiant with glittering gems ; and the mind is almost overwhelmed with the combined effects of excessive brilliancy and excessive grandeur. But such a scene cannot be described.

*   *   *

" From age to age—in winter's frost, or summer's sultry beam,
  By day, by night, without a pause—thy waves with loud acclaim,
  In ceaseless sounds, have still proclaimed the Great Eternal Name."

Our View is taken from the Canadian side, a short distance above Prospect House.

NIAGARA BY MOONLIGHT.

It were vain to attempt a description of this magical scene. Every one knows the peculiar softness and the sweet influence of moonlight shed over a lovely scene. Let not the traveller fail to visit Goat Island when the moon shines high and clear, and view Niagara by her pale, mysterious light.

LEGEND OF THE WHITE CANOE.

In days of old, long before the deep solitudes of the West were disturbed by white men, it was the custom of the Indian warriors of the forest to assemble at the Great Cataract and offer a human sacrifice to the Spirit of the Falls. The offering consisted of a white canoe

full of ripe fruits and blooming flowers, which was pad-
dled over the terrible cliff by the fairest girl of the tribe
who had just arrived at the age of womanhood. It was
counted an honour by the tribe to whose lot it fell to
make the costly sacrifice; and even the doomed maiden
deemed it a high compliment to be selected to guide
the white canoe over the Falls. But in the Stoical heart
of the red man there are tender feelings which cannot be
subdued, and cords which snap if strained too roughly.

The only daughter of a chief of the Seneca Indians
was chosen as a sacrificial offering to the Spirit of Niagara. Her mother had been slain by a hostile tribe.
Her father was the bravest among the warriors, and his
stern brow seldom relaxed save to his blooming child,
who was now the only joy to which he clung on earth.
When the lot fell on his fair child no symptom of feeling crossed his countenance. In the pride of Indian
endurance he crushed down the feelings that tore his
bosom, and no tear trembled in his dark eye as the pre-
parations for the sacrifice went forward. At length the
day arrived; it faded into night as the savage festivities
and rejoicing proceeded ; then the moon arose and sil-
vered the cloud of mist that rose from out the turmoil
of Niagara; and now the white canoe, laden with its
precious freight, glided from the bank and swept out
into the dread rapid from which escape is hopeless.
The young girl calmly steered her tiny bark towards the

centre of the stream, while frantic yells and shouts arose from the forest. Suddenly *another* white canoe shot forth upon the stream, and, under the powerful impulse of the Seneca chief, flew like an arrow to destruction. It overtook the first; the eyes of father and child met in one last gaze of love, and, then, they plunged together over the thundering cataract into eternity!

OBJECTS OF INTEREST IN THE NEIGHBOUR-HOOD OF THE FALLS.

The Falls of Niagara will doubtless occupy nearly all the time and engross all the interest of visitors; nevertheless there are several objects in the vicinity which are worthy of special attention. In enumerating these, we will adopt the plan of beginning at the cataract and descending to Lake Ontario; afterwards we will describe the river from Lake Erie to the Falls. The first object of interest below the cataract is

THE NIAGARA SUSPENSION BRIDGE,

Which spans the river about two miles below the Falls. We may mention, in passing, that there are two caves— *Catlin's Cave* and the *Giant's Cave*—between the Bridge and the Falls, on the American side; and *Bender's Cave* on the Canada side. They are, however, hardly worthy of notice.

The Suspension Bridge is a noble and stupendous

6

structure. It is the work of Mr. John A. Roebling of
Trenton, New Jersey, and was begun in 1852. Formerly
the bridge here was of much smaller dimensions. It
was begun in 1849 by Mr. Charles Elliot, who first
crossed it in an iron basket, slung under a single cable
of iron wire. Afterwards many people crossed in this
way, being let down the incline and drawn up on the
opposite side by a windlass. While six workmen were
employed on the foot-path of this bridge, a terrific gale
burst upon them, tore the planks away, and left four of
their number clinging to two thin wires, which swung
fearfully to and fro, while the whirling rapids raged
beneath them. The other two escaped on fragments of
board to the shore. A brave comrade descended in the
basket, during a lull in the gale, and by means of a ladder rescued his companions from their awful position.
The basket is still to be seen on the Canada side.

The present bridge is of enormous strength, and forms
a communication between Canada and the States, over
which the carriages of the Great Western and the New
York Central Railroads, and cars of every description,
run without causing the slightest vibration. The cost
of its construction was 500,000 dollars (more than
£100,000 sterling); and steam carriages first crossed it
on the 8th March 1855. The road for carriages is suspended 28 feet below the railway line.

The following statistics of this enormous bridge will

NIAGARA SUSPENSION BRIDGE.

be interesting: The height of the towers on the American side is 88 feet; those on the Canada side are 78 feet high. Length of bridge is 800 feet; width, 24 feet; height above the river, 250 feet. There are four enormous wire cables of about 10 inches diameter, which contain about 4000 miles of wire; and the ultimate capacity of the four cables is about 12,400 tons. The total weight of the bridge is 800 tons; and it combines, in an eminent degree, strength with elegance of structure. Our Engraving is from a photograph.

LUNDY'S LANE BATTLE-GROUND

Is about a mile and a half from the Falls, near to Clifton House. This great battle between the Americans and the British was fought on the 25th July 1814. The number of killed and wounded on both sides was about equal, and both parties, as a matter of course, claim the victory!

Drummondville, in the immediate vicinity, is named after General Drummond, then commander of the British forces.

Niagara City stands on either side of the Suspension Bridge, but it is not as yet deserving of the title of a city.

THE WHIRLPOOL.

About three miles below the Falls the river takes an abrupt turn, and shoots with great violence against the cliff on the Canada side, forming what is called the

Whirlpool. Our Engraving is from a drawing by the graphic pencil of Mr. Friend. The scenery around this caldron is exceedingly wild.

A short distance farther on are the *Mineral Springs,* sometimes called the Belle Vue Fountain.

The Rapids, just below the Whirlpool, are very fine.

Less than half a mile farther down the river, on the American side, is

THE DEVIL'S HOLE,

A terribly gloomy and savage chasm in the bank of the river, between one and two hundred feet deep. Overhanging this dark cavern is a perpendicular precipice, from the top of which falls a small stream named the *Bloody Run.* The stream obtained its name from the following tragical incident:—

During the French war in 1763, a detachment of British soldiers (consisting of, some say 100, some 50 men,) was forwarded with a large supply of provisions from Fort Niagara to Fort Schlosser. The Seneca Indians, then in the pay of the French, resolved to lay an ambuscade for them, and chose this dark spot for their enterprise. The savages, who were numerous, scattered themselves along the hill sides, and lay concealed among the bushes until the British came up and had passed the precipice; then, uttering a terrific yell, they descended like a whirlwind, and, before the soldiers had time to

WHIRLPOOL NEAR NIAGARA.

form, poured into their confused ranks a withering vol-
ley of bullets. The little stream ran red with blood,
and the whole party—soldiers, waggons, horses, and
drivers—were hurled over the cliff into the yawning
gulf below, and dashed to pieces on the rocks. Only
two escaped to tell the tale; the one a soldier, who re-
turned during the night to Fort Niagara ; the other a
Mr. Stedman, who dashed his horse through the ranks
of his enemies, and escaped amid a shower of bullets.

The Ice Cave is also an object of attraction in this
locality.

Chasm Tower is a short distance below. It is 75 feet
high, and affords a fine view of the river and surrounding scenery.

BROCK'S MONUMENT

Stands on the Queenston Heights, Canada side, just
above the village of that name. This monument was
raised in commemoration of the British General, Sir
Isaac Brock, who fell in the sanguinary action fought on
this spot on the 13th October 1812. His remains, and
those of his aid-de-camp, Colonel John M'Donald, who
died of wounds received in the same battle, are buried here.

The first monument was completed in 1826, and was
blown up in 1840 by a person named Lett, who was
afterwards imprisoned for this dastardly act. The present handsome shaft was erected in 1853. Its height

is 185 feet; the base is 40 feet square by 30 feet high; the shaft is of freestone, fluted, 75 feet high and 30 feet in circumference, surmounted by a Corinthian capital, on which stands a statue of the gallant General.

The view from this monument is most gorgeous. The eye wanders with untiring delight over the richest imaginable scene of woodland and water. Just below is the village of Queenston, and on the opposite shore is Lewiston. In the midst flows the now tranquil River Niagara—calm and majestic in its recovered serenity. In the far distance, on either side, stretches the richly wooded landscape, speckled with villas and cottages. At the mouth of the river are the town of *Niagara* on the Canadian side, and *Youngstown* on the American. Its entrance is guarded on the latter side by *Fort Niagara*, and on the former by *Fort Massasauga*. The whole view is terminated by the magnificent sheet of Lake Ontario, which stretches away like a flood of light to the horizon.

QUEENSTON

Is a small picturesque town, and worthy of notice chiefly on account of the memorable battle that took place on the neighbouring heights.

LEWISTON,

Just opposite Queenston, is a beautifully situated town, about seven miles from the Falls. It is a place of some

Brock's Monument

importance, and stands at the head of the navigation on the river; contains several excellent hotels and public buildings. The Buffalo, Niagara Falls, and Lewiston Railroad terminus, is here. There is a village of Tuscarora Indians three miles from this. Lewiston was destroyed by the British in 1813, and rebuilt at the termination of the war.

Just above those two towns is the

LEWISTON SUSPENSION BRIDGE.

This is the finest bridge of the kind in America. It was erected in 1850 by E. W. Serrell, Esq., of Canada, and belongs to a joint company of Americans and Canadians. Its length is 1045 feet; and it is suspended by ten massive cables, which pass over stone towers, and are attached to anchors imbedded deep in the solid rock.

NIAGARA TOWN

Stands on the Canada shore, opposite Youngstown, on the site of Newark, which was burnt in 1813 by General M'Clure. Its prosperity has been injured somewhat by the Welland Canal. A short distance above the town are the remains of *Fort George*, which was taken by the Americans in 1813, afterwards destroyed by the British, and left in ruins.

Fort Niagara, on the American side, has many historical associations, which we have not space to touch upon. The English General Prideaux fell here in the battle of 24th July 1759, and the French garrison afterwards surrendered to Sir William Johnson.

Fort Massasauga, at the mouth of the river, opposite Fort Niagara, is a little below the town of Niagara, and is garrisoned by British soldiers.

NIAGARA RIVER ABOVE THE FALLS.

Having now traced this noble river from the Falls to its mouth, let us proceed to its source at Lake Erie, and give it a rapid glance as we follow its course to the great cataract.

Buffalo, at its commencement, stands guard at the outlet of Lake Erie. This is a great commercial city, from which trains leave daily for all parts of the States and Canada. Railway direct to the Falls, which are distant about 22 miles. The terminus of this railway is at Lewiston, and it connects with the Great Western Railway of Canada at the Suspension Bridge. Just opposite is old *Fort Erie*, belonging to the British.

Black Rock, now part of Buffalo, once rivalled that city in importance. Here a steam-ferry crosses over to *Waterloo*, a village on the Canada shore.

Tonawanda is 12 miles from Buffalo, at the widest part of Niagara River.

Grand Island, on which is a little hamlet named *White Haven*, divides the river into two branches. On the site of White Haven was intended to be built a " city of refuge for the Jews;" but the aspiring and sanguine projector failed in carrying out his intention.

Fort Schlosser is 9 miles farther down the river, on the American side. It was at the old landing here that the *burning of the Caroline* took place, during the Canadian rebellion in 1837.

The insurgents had taken up a position on *Navy Island*, and the Caroline steamer was charged by the British with carrying provisions to the rebels. The vessel was therefore seized by Colonel M'Nabb, cut loose from her moorings, set on fire, and sent, like a flaming meteor, down the wild rapids and over the Falls of Niagara. There was no one on board when this vessel took her awful leap into the roaring gulf. Opposite Schlosser is the village of *Chippewa* (2½ miles above the Falls), from which a railway runs to Queenston and the mouth of the river. Steamers ply between Buffalo and this village, below which vessels dare not venture.

THE ISLANDS

Above the rapids are very numerous. Indeed, the river is studded with them, from Lake Erie all the way down to the Falls. There are 37 of them, if we may be permitted to count those that are little more than large rocks. *Grand Island* is the largest, being 12 miles long and 7 broad. It divides the stream into two

D

branches. *Navy Island* is just below it. Here the French built their ships of war in 1759. This island was the resort of the rebel leaders in 1837. It has an area of 304 acres. Our space forbids further notice of these islands, which are exquisitely beautiful. Some are large, and others are small ; some lie in quiet water, clearly reflected in the surrounding mirror ; while others stand in the midst of the raging current, looking black in the white turmoil of surrounding foam, and seeming as if they would fain check the angry waters in their headlong rush towards the Falls.

There is a fascination about this mighty cataract which seems to chain us to the spot, and, when we seek to leave it, draws us irresistibly back again. Even in describing it, however inadequately the task may be accomplished, we are loath to lay down the pen and tear ourselves away. The Almighty has invested Niagara with a power which none can resist; and those who gaze upon it for the first time, have a new era in their existence opened up—new thoughts and impressions stamped indelibly on their hearts, which will haunt them in after years and linger on their memories till these hearts and memories cease to act, and time is swallowed in eternity.

GEOLOGY OF NIAGARA.

THE geological features of the district around Niagara are very remarkable, and the Falls afford a fine example of the power of water to form an excavation of great depth and considerable length in the solid rock. The country over which the river flows is a flat table-land, elevated about 330 feet above Lake Ontario. Lake Erie, situated in a depression of this platform, is about 36 miles distant from Ontario, lying to the south-west. This table-land extends towards Queenston, where it terminates suddenly in an abrupt line of cliff, or escarpment, facing towards the north. The land then continues on a lower level to Lake Ontario.

The descent of the River Niagara—which, let it be borne in remembrance, flows *northward*—is only about fifteen feet in the first fifteen miles from Lake Erie, and the country around is almost on a level with the river's banks. At this part the Niagara varies from one to three miles in width, has a tranquil current, and is lake-like in appearance, being interspersed with low, wooded islands. At the head of the rapids it assumes a totally different appearance, and descends about fifty feet in less than a mile, over an uneven bed of lime-

stone, and, after being divided into two sheets by Goat
Island, plunges down about 164 feet perpendicular at
the Falls.   Just below the Falls the river narrows
abruptly, and flows rapidly through a deep gorge, vary-
ing from 200 to 400 yards wide, and 300 feet deep. This
gorge, or chasm, extends from the Falls to the escarpment above referred to, near Queenston, a distance of
seven miles; in the course of which the river descends
100 feet, and then emerges on the low, level land lying
between the Queenston Heights and Lake Ontario,—a
farther distance of seven miles.   The descent here is
only about four feet altogether, and the flow of the river
is placid.   The chasm is winding in form, and, about
the centre of its course, makes a turn nearly at right
angles, forming the well-known whirlpool.

Such are the various appearances and peculiarities
presented by the River and Falls of Niagara, the causes
of which we shall endeavour to explain.

The escarpment at Queenston, and the sides of the
great ravine, have enabled us in the most satisfactory
manner to ascertain the geological formations of the district, and to account for the present position of the
Falls, as well as to form, on good grounds, an opinion as
to the probable working of this mighty cataract in the
future.   It has long been supposed that the Falls
originally plunged over the cliff at Queenston, and that
they have gradually eaten their way back, a distance of

seven miles, to their present position. It is further conjectured that they will continue to cut their way back, in the course of ages, to Lake Erie, and that an extensive inundation will be caused by the waters of the lake thus set free. Recent investigation has shown, however, that this result is highly improbable,—we may almost say impossible; that the peculiar quality and position of the strata over which the river flows are such, that the Falls will be diminished in height as they recede, and their recession be checked altogether at a certain point.

It has been ascertained beyond all doubt that the Falls do recede, but the rate of this retrograde movement is very uncertain, and, indeed, we have every reason to believe that the rate of recession must of necessity in time past have been *irregular*. The cause of this irregularity becomes apparent on considering the formations presented to view at the escarpent and in the chasm. Here we find that the strata are nearly horizontal, as indeed they are throughout the whole region, having a very slight dip towards the south of twenty-five feet in a mile. They all consist of different members of the Silurian series, and vary considerably in thickness and density. In consequence of the slight dip in the strata, above referred to, the different groups of rock crop out from beneath each other, and thus appear on the surface in parallel zones or belts; and the Falls, in their retrograde movement, after cutting through one of these zones, would meet with another of a totally different character; having cut through which, a third would succeed, and so on.

In all probability Niagara originally flowed through a shallow valley, similar to that above the Falls, all the way across the table-land to the Queenston heights, or escarpment. On this point Sir C. Lyell writes: "I obtained geological evidence of the former existence of an old river-bed, which, I have no doubt, indicates the original channel through which the waters once flowed from the Falls to Queenston, at the height of nearly 300 feet above the bottom of the present gorge. The geological monuments alluded to consist of patches of sand and gravel, forty feet thick, containing fluviatile shells of the genera Unio, Cyclas, Melania, &c., such as now inhabit the waters of the Niagara above the Falls. The identity of the fossil species with the recent is unquestionable, and these fresh-water deposits occur at the edge of the cliffs bounding the ravine, so that they prove the former extension of an elevated shallow valley, four miles below the Falls,—a distinct prolongation of that now occupied by the Niagara in the elevated region between Lake Erie and the Falls."

At the escarpment the cataract thundered over a precipice twice the height of the present one, to the lower level. This lower level, as shown by Hall's Report on the Geology of New York, is composed of red shaly sandstone and marl. The formations incumbent upon this, exhibited on the face of the escarpment, are as follow: 1. Gray quartzose sandstone; 2. Red shaly sandstone, similar to that of the low level, with thin courses of sandstone near the top; 3. Gray mottled sandstone; 4. A thin bed of green shale; 5. Compact gray limestone; 6. A thick stratum of soft argillo-calcareous shale, similar to that which now lies at the base of the Falls; 7. A thick stratum of limestone, compact and geodiferous, similar to the limestone rock which forms the upper part of the Falls. This is all that we have presented to us in the escarpment; but we may observe, parenthetically, that if we proceed backwards towards Lake Erie, we cross the zone of limestone, and at the Falls discover another stratum of thin-bedded limestone overlapping it, in consequence of the southerly dip before referred to. Farther back still we find the Onondaga salt group, which extends, superficially, almost to Lake Erie, where another limestone formation appears.

Now, had there been no dip in the strata of the table-land between Lake Erie and Queenston, it is probable that the Falls would have continued to recede *regularly*, having always the same formations to cut through, and the same foundation to fall upon and excavate. But in consequence of the gentle inclination of the strata to the south, the surface presented to the action of the Falls has continually varied, and the process of recession has been as follows :—

First, the river, rolling over the upper formation of hard limestone, to the escarpment, thundered down a height about double that of the present Fall, and struck upon the red shaly sandstone of the plain below. This being soft, was rapidly worn away by the action of the water and spray, while the more compact rocks above, comparatively unaffected, projected over the caldron, and at length fell in masses from time to time as the undermining process went on. But, as the Falls receded, the belt of red sandstone was gradually crossed, and the gray quartzose sandstone became the foundation of the group, and the recipient of Niagara's tremendous blows. This rock is extremely hard ; here, therefore, the retrograde movement was probably retarded for ages ; and here, just at the point where the Falls intersected this thin stratum of quartzose sandstone, the whirlpool is now situated.

The next formation on which the Falls operated was the red shaly sandstone, similar to the first ; which, being soft, accelerated the recession. This went on at increased speed until the stratum was cut through, and the third formation was reached. Here again an alteration in speed occurred as before. The last that has been cut through is the fifth stratum, compact gray limestone, on which the cataract now falls.

The formation now reached, and that on which Niagara is operating at the present day, is the soft argillo-calcareous shale. It extends from the bottom of the precipice, over which the water plunges, to nearly half way up, and is about eighty feet thick. Above it lies the compact refractory limestone, which forms the upper formation at this point. This also is about eighty feet thick; and here we see the process of excavation progressing rapidly. The lower stratum, being soft, is disintegrated by the violent action of the water and spray, aided in winter by frost; and portions of the incumbent rock, being thus left unsupported, fall down from time to time. The huge masses of undermined limestone that fell in the years 1818 and 1828, shook the country, it is said, like an earthquake.

This process is continually altering the appearance of the Falls. Sir Charles Lyell, in his geological treatise on this region, says: "According to the statement of our guide in 1841, (Samuel Hooker,) an indentation of about forty feet has been produced in the middle of the ledge of limestone at the lesser Fall since the year 1815, so that it has begun to assume the shape of a crescent; while within the same period the Horse-Shoe Fall has been altered so as less to deserve its name. Goat Island has lost several acres in area in the last four years; and I have no doubt that this waste neither is, nor has been, a mere temporary accident, since I found that the same

8

recession was in progress in various other waterfalls which I visited with Mr. Hall in the State of New York."

The rate at which the Falls now recede is a point of dispute. Mr. Bakewell calculated that, in the forty years preceding 1830, Niagara had been going back at the rate of about a yard annually. Sir Charles Lyell, on the other hand, is of opinion that one foot per annum is a much more probable conjecture. As we have already explained, this rapid rate of recession has, in all likelihood, not been uniform, but that in many parts of its course Niagara has remained almost stationary for ages.

That the Falls will ever reach Lake Erie is rendered extremely improbable from the following facts : Owing to the formation of the land, they are gradually losing in height, and, therefore, in power, as they retreat. Moreover, we know that, in consequence of the southerly dip of the strata, they will have cut through the bed of soft shale after travelling two miles farther back ; thus the massive limestone which is now at the top will then be at the bottom of the precipice, while, at the same time, the Falls will be only half their present height. This latter hypothesis has been advanced by Mr. Hall, who, in his survey, has demonstrated that there is a diminution of forty feet in the perpendicular height of the Falls for every mile that they recede southwards ; and this conclusion is based upon two facts, namely, that the slope of the river-channel, in its course northward, is fifteen feet in a mile, and that the dip of the strata in an opposite, or southerly direction, is about twenty-five feet in a mile.

From this it seems probable that, in the course of between ten and eleven thousand years, the Falls of Niagara, having the thick and hard limestone at their base, and having diminished to half their present height, will be effectually retarded in their retrograde progress, if not previously checked by the fall of large masses of the rock from the cliff above. Should they still recede, however, beyond this point, in the course of future ages they will have to intersect entirely different strata from that over which they now fall, and will be so diminished in height as to be almost lost before reaching Lake Erie.

The question as to the origin of the Falls,—the manner in which they commenced, and the geological period at which they first came into existence,—is one of great interest; but want of space forbids our discussing that question here. We can make but one or two brief remarks in regard to it.

Sir Charles Lyell is of opinion that originally the whole country was beneath the surface of the ocean, at a very remote geological period; that it emerged slowly from the sea, and was again submerged at a comparatively modern period, when shells then inhabiting the ocean belonged almost without exception to species still living in high northern latitudes, and some of them in temperate latitudes. The next great change was the slow and gradual re-emergence of this country.

As soon as the table-land between Lakes Erie and Ontario emerged, the River Niagara came into existence; and at the same moment there was a cascade of moderate height at Queenston, which fell directly into the sea. The cataract then commenced its retrograde movement. As the land slowly emerged, and the hard beds were exposed, another Fall would be formed; and then probably a third, when the quartzose sandstone appeared. The recession of the uppermost Fall must have been retarded by the thick limestone bed through which it had to cut; the second Fall, not being exposed to the same hinderance, overtook it; and thus the three ultimately came to be joined in one.

The successive ages that must have rolled on, during the evolution of these events, are beyond the power of the human intellect to appreciate, and belong to those " deep things " of the great Creator, whose ways are infinitely above our finite comprehension. It is roughly calculated that the Falls must have taken at least 35,000 years to cut their way from the escarpment of Queenston to their present position; yet this period, great though it is in comparison with the years to which the annals of the human race are limited, is as nothing when compared with the previous ages whose extent is indicated by the geological formations in the region around Niagara.

POETICAL LINES.

TO NIAGARA.

WRITTEN AT THE FIRST SIGHT OF ITS FALLS,
August 13, 1837.

HAIL! Sovereign of the world of floods! whose majesty and might
First dazzles, then enraptures, then o'erawes the aching sight:
The pomp of kings and emperors, in every clime and zone,
Grows dim beneath the splendour of thy glorious watery throne.

No fleets can stop thy progress, no armies bid thee stay,
But onward,—onward,—onward,—thy march still holds its way;
The rising mists that veil thee as thy heralds go before,
And the music that proclaims thee is the thund'ring cataract's roar.

Thy diadem's an emerald, of the clearest, purest hue,
Set round with waves of snow-white foam, and spray of feathery dew;
While tresses of the brightest pearls float o'er thine ample sheet,
And the rainbow lays its gorgeous gems in tribute at thy feet.

Thy reign is from the ancient days, thy sceptre from on high;
Thy birth was when the distant stars first lit the glowing sky;
The sun, the moon, and all the orbs that shine upon thee now,
Beheld the wreath of glory which first bound thine infant brow

And from that hour to this, in which I gaze upon thy stream,
From age to age, in Winter's frost or Summer's sultry beam,
By day, by night, without a pause, thy waves, with loud acclaim,
In ceaseless sounds have still proclaim'd the Great Eternal's name.

For whether, on thy forest banks, the Indian of the wood,
Or, since his day, the red man's foe on his fatherland has stood;
Whoe'er has seen thine incense rise, or heard thy torrents roar,
Must have knelt before the God of all, to worship and adore.

Accept, then, O Supremely Great! O Infinite! O God!
From this primeval altar, the green and virgin sod,
The humble homage that my soul in gratitude would pay
To Thee whose shield has guarded me through all my wandering way.

For if the ocean be as nought in the hollow of thine hand,
And the stars of the bright firmament in thy balance grains of sand;
If Niagara's rolling flood seems great to us who humbly bow,
O Great Creator of the Whole, how passing great art Thou!

But though thy power is far more vast than finite mind can scan,
Thy mercy is still greater shown to weak, dependent man:
For him thou cloth'st the fertile globe with herbs, and fruit, and seed;
For him the seas, the lakes, the streams, supply his hourly need.

Around, on high, or far, or near, the universal whole
Proclaims thy glory, as the orbs in their fixed courses roll;
And from creation's grateful voice the hymn ascends above,
While heaven re-echoes back to earth the chorus—" God is love."

                                            J. S. BUCKINGHAM.

THE FALLS OF NIAGARA.

THERE'S nothing great or bright, thou glorious Fall!
Thou mayst not to the fancy's sense recall—
The thunder-riven cloud, the lightning's leap,
The stirrings of the chambers of the deep—
Earth's emerald green and many-tinted dyes,
The fleecy whiteness of the upper skies,
The tread of armies thickening as they come,
The boom of cannon and the beat of drum,
The brow of beauty and the form of grace,
The passion and the prowess of our race,
The song of Homer in its loftiest hour,
The unresisting sweep of Roman power,
Britannia's trident on the azure sea,
America's young shout of liberty!

Oh, may the wars that madden on these deeps,
There spend their rage, nor climb the encircling steeps;
And till the conflict of their surges cease
The nations on thy banks repose in peace!

                                            LORD MORPETH.

NIAGARA.

FLOW on for ever, in thy glorious robe
Of terror and of beauty. Yea, flow on,
Unfathom'd and resistless. God hath set
His rainbow on thy forehead, and the cloud
Mantled around thy feet. And He doth give
Thy voice of thunder power to speak of Him
Eternally—bidding the lip of man
Keep silence, and upon thine altar pour
Incense of awe-struck praise.
                    Earth fears to lift
The insect trump that tells her trifling joys
Or fleeting triumphs, 'mid the peal sublime
Of thy tremendous hymn. Proud Ocean shrinks
Back from thy brotherhood, and all his waves
Retire abash'd. For he hath need to sleep,
Sometimes, like a spent labourer, calling home
His boisterous billows, from their vexing play,
To a long dreary calm: but thy strong tide
Faints not, nor e'er with failing heart forgets
Its everlasting lesson, night nor day.
The morning stars, that hail'd creation's birth,
Heard thy hoarse anthem mixing with their song,
Jehovah's name; and the dissolving fires,
That wait the mandate of the day of doom   .
To wreck the earth, shall find it deep inscribed
Upon thy rocky scroll.
      *   *   *   *
                    Lo! yon birds,
How bold! they venture near, dipping their wing
In all thy mist and foam. Perchance 'tis meet
For them to touch thy garment's hem, or stir
Thy diamond wreath, who sport upon the cloud
Unblamed, or warble at the gate of heaven
Without reproof. But as for us, it seems

Scarce lawful with our erring lips to talk
Familiarly of thee.   Methinks, to trace
Thine awful features with our pencil's point
Were but to press on Sinai.
               Thou dost speak
Alone of God, who pour'd thee as a drop
From His right hand—bidding the soul that looks
Upon thy fearful majesty be still,
Be humbly wrapp'd in its own nothingness,
And lose itself in Him.

                          SIGOURNEY.

THE FALLS OF NIAGARA.

THE thoughts are strange that crowd into my brain
While I look upward to thee.   It would seem
As if God poured thee from his "hollow hand,"
And hung his bow upon thine awful front,
And spoke in that loud voice which seemed to him
Who dwelt in Patmos for his Saviour's sake,
" The sound of many waters ;" and had bade
Thy flood to chronicle the ages back,
And notch the centuries in the eternal rocks.
Deep calleth unto deep.   And what are we,
That hear the question of that voice sublime?
Oh ! what are all the notes that ever rung
From war's vain trumpet, by thy thundering side?
Yea, what is all the riot that man makes
In his short life, to thy unceasing roar?
And yet, bold babbler, what art thou to Him
Who drowned a world, and heaped the waters far
Above its loftiest mountains ?—a light wave
That breaks and whispers of its Maker's might !

                          BRAINARD.

www.ingramcontent.com/pod-product-compliance
Lightning Source LLC
Chambersburg PA
CBHW021425090426
42742CB00009B/1260